SMART WORDS
READER

INSECTS
and
SPIDERS

Christine A. Caputo

SCHOLASTIC INC.

What are SMART WORDS?

Smart Words are frequently used words that are critical to understanding concepts taught in the classroom. The more Smart Words a child knows, the more easily he or she will grasp important curriculum concepts. Smart Words Readers introduce these key words in a fun and motivational format while developing important literacy skills. Each new word is highlighted, defined in context, and reviewed. Engaging activities at the end of each chapter allow readers to practice the words they have learned.

ISBN 978-0-545-46703-2

Packaged by Q2A Bill Smith

Copyright © 2012 by Scholastic Inc.

Picture Credit: t= top, b= bottom, l= left, r= right, c= center

Cover Page: Eric Isselee/Shutterstock, Enciktat/Shutterstock.
Title Page: Rob Hainer/Shutterstock.
Contents Page: Nico99/Shutterstock.

4: Norbert Wu/Science Faction/Terra/Corbis; 5: George Grall/National Geographic Society/National Geographic/Corbis; 6: Henrik Larsson/Shutterstock; 7: Monkeystock/Shutterstock; 8c: Volodymyr/Shutterstock; 8b: Wetchawut/Shutterstock; 9: Kuttelvaserova/Shutterstock; 12: Woewchikyury/Istockphoto; 13: Image100/Corbis; 14c: Fong Kam Yee/Shutterstock; 14b: Lucian Coman/Shutterstock; 15: Cathy Keifer/Shutterstock; 16: Craig Tuttle/Terra/Corbis; 17: Robert Marien/Corbis Yellow/Corbis; 18: kurt_G/Shutterstock; 19: Kletr/Shutterstock; 20: EcoPrint/Shutterstock; 21: Audrey Snider-Bell/Shutterstock; 24: Keith Naylor/Shutterstock; 25: Daniel Prudek/Shutterstock; 26: Peteri/Shutterstock; 27: Yuttasak Jannarong/Shutterstock; 28: Romantsova Olga/Shutterstock; 29: Esther Beaton/Encyclopedia/Corbis.

Q2A Bill Smith Art Bank: Title Page, 10-11, 23.

12 11 10   16 17/0

Printed in the U.S.A.   40
First printing, September 2012

Table of Contents

Chapter 1

Irresistible Insects

Look around you. Look closer. Closer. There! A tiny parade of ants marches in a row carrying food back to their mound. A hive of bees busily makes a batch of honey. A grasshopper chews on a leaf.

Ants, bees, grasshoppers, and other insects all share some specific characteristics, or traits. Let's find out more about these traits!

Army ants work in groups to find food.

How to Spot an insect

Look for these traits:
- does not have a backbone
- has an exoskeleton
- has a body usually with three segments
- has two antennae
- has three pairs of legs
- usually has two pairs of wings

An insect is an **invertebrate**, which means it does not have a backbone. Instead, an insect has a hard covering on the outside of its body called an **exoskeleton**. This shell-like structure protects and supports the soft parts inside the insect's body. It also keeps water inside so the insect won't dry out.

exoskeleton

This insect has shed its exoskeleton. An insect may have several different exoskeletons in its lifetime.

The exoskeleton doesn't grow as the insect gets bigger. The insect grows out of its exoskeleton. It leaves the old exoskeleton behind and forms a new one. This process is known as molting.

SMART WORDS

insect an invertebrate animal that has a body with usually three segments, an exoskeleton, three pairs of legs, two antennae, and usually two pairs of wings

invertebrate an animal without a backbone

exoskeleton a hard covering on the outside of an animal's body

Insect Bodies

Most insects' bodies have three basic segments, or parts: the head, thorax, and abdomen. The head is at one end of the body. The insect's mouth and eyes are on its head the same way yours are. But an insect has something on its head that you don't. Most insects have two **antennae**, which are long, thin structures used for feeling and smelling. They can look like strings, feathers, threads, or even beads.

antennae head thorax wing abdomen

antennae

head

t

wing

abdomen

The middle part of an insect's body is the tho
t helps the insect to move. An insect's six le
on its thorax. Each leg has a joint where it ca
ts wings are on the thorax, too. An adult inse
usually has two pairs of wings.

The **abdomen** is generally the largest part of
nsect's body. It contains all the parts the inse
o digest food and to produce young. The ab
also has small openings on it that let air mov
he insect. This is how the insect breathes!

SMART WORDS

antennae long, thin structures on an insect's
head that are used for feeling and smelling

thorax the middle part of an insect's body that
has legs and wings attached to it

abdomen the part of an insect's body that helps
it digest food, produce young, and breathe

The Better to See You With

All insects have **compound eyes**. They are made up of hundreds or thousands of separate parts that work together. Compound eyes let an insect see very clearly all around — but for only a short distance. They help an insect zip through plants and trees without crashing into them.

Each one of a dragonfly's eyes has about 30,000 parts.

The butterfly uses a tube-like structure on its head to sip liquid out of a flower or a piece of rotting fruit.

The Better to Eat You With

When you chew your food, your jaw moves up and down. Your teeth and tongue help break down the food so you can swallow it. But when an insect chews, its jaws move from side to side. Insects have different mouthparts depending on the type of food they eat.

Some insects, like butterflies, have mouthparts that let them slurp up their food like they are using a straw. Others, like ants, have mouthparts that help them hold, tear apart, and carry their food. A few types, including thrips, have sandpaper-like mouthparts. They scratch the surface of a plant and then suck up any liquids that leak out.

SMART WORD

compound eye a structure made up of many separate parts that helps an animal see

Growing Up

You have changed a lot since you were born. You've gotten bigger. You look older. You may have more hair. Insects also change as they grow. All of the changes that an animal goes through from the time it is born until it can produce young is known as its **life cycle**. This diagram shows the life cycle of a butterfly. The adult butterfly looks completely different from the young butterfly.

Egg
A female butterfly lays a tiny egg on a leaf or a plant.

Larva
In about a week, the egg develops into a wormlike creature called a caterpillar. The caterpillar eats and eats until it grows several times its original size.

Pupa
A few weeks later, the caterpillar becomes wrapped in a structure known as a chrysalis. Inside, the caterpillar is changing in form.

Adult
After several weeks, the chrysalis splits open and a colorful butterfly comes out. The butterfly shakes its wings and flies away.

Not all animals have the same life cycle. For example, this adult grasshopper looks a lot like the young grasshopper. The main change is that the adult grasshopper has wings.

Egg
A female grasshopper lays a group of eggs in a hole. She covers them with a sticky substance that protects them.

Adult
After about 4 to 7 weeks, the grasshopper is an adult. Unlike the butterfly, the grasshopper does not have a major change in form.

Nymph
After about two weeks, a young grasshopper forms from an egg. It looks like an adult grasshopper, but it doesn't have wings. As it grows, it molts several times and slowly forms wings.

SMART WORD

life cycle the changes an animal goes through from the time it is born until it can produce young

Match each description to the correct Smart Word.

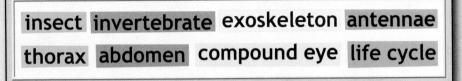

insect invertebrate exoskeleton antennae
thorax abdomen compound eye life cycle

1. a part of an insect's body that has legs and wings
2. a structure made up of many separate parts that helps an animal see
3. a part of an insect's body that helps it digest food and breathe
4. the changes an insect goes through from the time it is born until it can produce young
5. any animal without a backbone
6. a hard covering on the outside of the body of some animals
7. the parts on the insect's head that are used for touching and feeling
8. an animal without a backbone that has a body with usually three segments, a hard outer covering, three pairs of legs, two antennae, and usually two pairs of wings

Answers on page 32

Talk Like a Scientist

Suppose you are giving a tour at an insect museum, and someone on the tour asks you how the life cycle of a butterfly is different from the life cycle of a grasshopper. Use your Smart Words to answer the question.

SMART FACTS

Did You Know?

The stick insect gets its name because it looks just like a twig. It blends in with its surroundings to hide from other animals.

What a Trick!

Many stick insects pretend they are dead if they see an animal that might eat them. When the animal goes away, they suddenly "come back to life."

That's Amazing!

The smallest stick insects are about 0.5 inches (11.6 millimeters) long. The longest can be up to 21 inches (55 centimeters) long.

Chapter 2

Itsy-Bitsy Spider

Yikes! What's crawling near your foot? It's a **spider**! What exactly is a spider? Like insects, spiders are invertebrates with exoskeletons. Their bodies are also made up of segments. Unlike insects, however, spiders have just two body segments: a thorax and an abdomen.

How to Spot a spider

Look for these traits:

- does not have a backbone
- has an exoskeleton
- has eight legs
- has a body with two segments
- does not have wings or antennae

Spiders range in size from as small as your fingernail to about the size of your hand.

Most spiders can't see much except the difference between light and dark.

If you see an animal with eight legs, chances are you've found a spider. Spiders use all of their legs to walk, and some spiders can also use their two front legs to hold food. Unlike insects, spiders never have wings or antennae.

Spiders have simple eyes, but they often have eight of them! The pattern of eyes changes from one type of spider to another. Even with all those eyes, most spiders don't see as well as insects do. Instead, they use their senses of touch and taste to find their way around.

SMART WORD

spider an invertebrate that has a body with two segments, an exoskeleton, eight legs, and does not have wings or antennae

Weaving a Web

Spiders can't go to the grocery store to get food when they are hungry. Instead, they need to catch their dinner. That's the main reason why most spiders spin **webs**. Using pairs of spinning structures on their abdomens, spiders can make thin strands of silk. Different kinds of spiders spin different patterns. Most of the strands are sticky enough to catch any insects that happen to fly into the web.

The Darwin's bark spider makes the biggest round webs in the world. They can be over 82 feet (25 meters) across. That's the length of 14 bicycles lined up end-to-end!

Western black widow spiders build their webs close to the ground.

So what exactly do spiders eat? Most eat insects, like flies, wasps, and butterflies. Some large spiders, such as tarantulas, can eat lizards, frogs, and toads. Any animal that eats only meat is a **carnivore**.

Once a spider catches its food, it bites the animal with its sharp fangs. The fangs inject **venom** into the animal. Venom is a poison that spiders and some other animals make. It stuns or kills the animal and turns its body to a mushy liquid. As this happens, the spider wraps the animal's body in silk and then drinks the liquid.

SMART WORDS

web a net of silk threads that a spider uses to catch insects

carnivore an animal that eats only meat

venom poison produced by an animal

Baby Spiders

When it is time for a female spider to have babies, she lays **eggs**. Each egg contains the young spider along with food it needs as it develops.

The spider puts the eggs into an egg sac that is made from its silken thread. The sac protects the eggs from harm and from drying out. There can be as few as 4 or as many as 1,000 eggs in a single egg sac.

The female wolf spider can have up to 100 eggs at a time in her egg sac. She carries her egg sac to protect the young spiders.

Some females stay close by while the baby spiders hatch, but others leave and let the babies take care of themselves.

Some spiders place the egg sacs in a hole in the ground. Others hide them under tree bark or in a curled-up leaf. There are some spiders that hang them from a string of silk or in their own webs.

Once the young spiders are ready, they break out, or **hatch**, from their eggs. After a few days, they start to spread out in all directions in search of food.

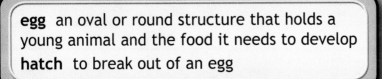

SMART WORDS

egg an oval or round structure that holds a young animal and the food it needs to develop

hatch to break out of an egg

Use your SMART WORDS

Answer each question with a Smart Word.

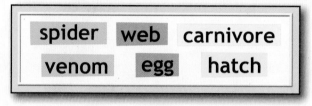

spider	web	carnivore
venom	egg	hatch

1. What is the name of a net made of silk that a spider uses to catch insects?

2. What does a spider do when it breaks out of its egg?

3. What term describes an animal that eats only meat?

4. What term describes a type of invertebrate that has a body with two segments, an exoskeleton, eight legs, and does not have wings or antennae?

5. What is a poisonous substance that a spider uses to stun or kill insects?

6. What is a structure that contains a young spider along with food it needs to develop?

Answers on page 32

Talk Like a Scientist

Write a paragraph for your school Web site explaining how spiders are different from insects. Use your Smart Words.

SMART FACTS

That's Amazing!

The Goliath bird-eating tarantula is one of the largest types of tarantulas in the world. Its legs can stretch across a 12-inch (30-centimeter) pizza.

Good to Know

As big as it is, this tarantula's venom is not deadly to humans. It can cause pain and an upset stomach, but a person bit by this spider will usually survive.

All That Noise!

This spider makes noise by rubbing its legs together. The noise is loud enough to be heard across a classroom.

Chapter 3

Crawling All Around

Where on Earth should you look to find an insect or a spider? The answer is: *Just about anywhere!* Insects and spiders live in all kinds of **ecosystems** on Earth. An ecosystem describes the living and nonliving things in an area. An ecosystem can be large, such as an entire forest, or small, such as a pond at the edge of the forest.

In every ecosystem, some living things eat other living things for food. A grasshopper might eat grass. A frog might eat the grasshopper. A snake might eat the frog and a hawk might eat the snake. This flow of food from one living thing to another is called a **food chain**.

Frogs eat grasshoppers, but birds and spiders eat grasshoppers, too. So grasshoppers can belong to more than one food chain at a time. In any ecosystem, several food chains can overlap to form a **food web**.

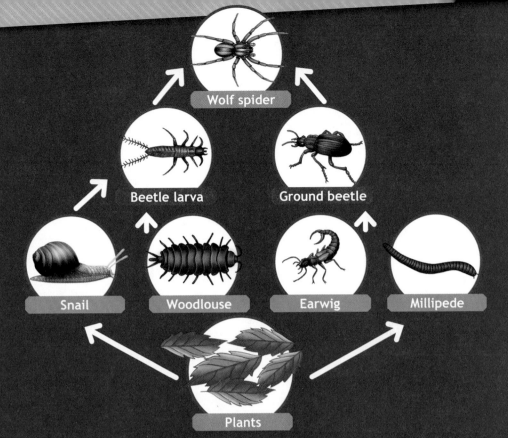

The diagram shows how two food chains form a food web. In the food chain on the left, the snail and the woodlouse eat the plants. The beetle larva eats the snail and the woodlouse. The wolf spider eats the beetle larva. In the food chain on the right, the earwig and the millipede eat the plants. The ground beetle eats the earwig and the millipede. The wolf spider eats the ground beetle.

SMART WORDS

ecosystem all of the living and nonliving things in an area

food chain the flow of food from one living thing to another

food web a group of overlapping food chains in a habitat

Keeping Balance

Do you think that insects and spiders do nothing but cause trouble? Think again! They actually help people more than they harm them. One way is by keeping the number of pests under control. A pest is any living thing that harms other living things or crops.

Aphids are pests that eat plants on farms. Ladybugs are insects that eat aphids. This stops the aphid population from getting too big and eating all the crops.

These hungry ladybugs are having a tasty aphid meal and saving the plant at the same time.

24

Bees pollinate apples, cucumbers, grapes, and many other fruits and vegetables.

Do you like to eat watermelon, broccoli, or apples? These are just a few of the plants that depend on insects for **pollination**.

In order for plants with flowers to make new plants, a powdery substance called pollen must be moved from one flower part to another. When an insect visits a flower to drink a sweet liquid known as nectar, some pollen sticks to the insect's body. When the insect moves on to another flower, some of the pollen falls off. In this way, the insect transfers the pollen.

SMART WORDS

pest any living thing that harms other living things or crops

pollination the movement of pollen from one flower part to another

Helping Out

Have you ever tasted honey? It's a thick, sweet liquid that people often use in cooking. Honey is produced by an insect known as the honeybee. Honeybees visit flowers to get nectar. Back at their hive, they use the nectar to make honey. The bees store the honey for winter. People, and sometimes animals such as bears, take the honey for a sweet treat.

Honeybees use wax from their bodies to make a honeycomb. They raise their young and store honey and pollen in the honeycomb cells.

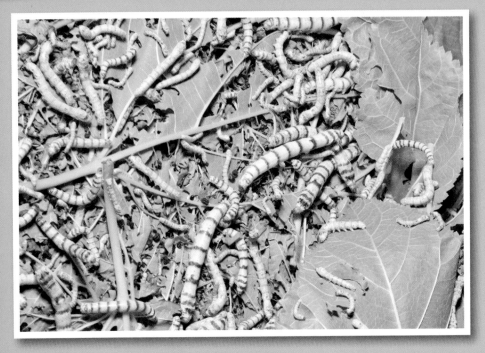

After these silkworms eat leaves for about six weeks, they will spin their cocoons.

Another type of insect has been at work for thousands of years — the silkworm! A silkworm is the larva stage of a certain type of moth. The silkworm, like some other insects, produces a covering called a **cocoon**. It's made out of one strand of silk that can be up to a mile long!

Since ancient times in China, people have been unwinding these cocoons and using the threads to make beautiful silk fabrics. Silk threads are also used in bicycle tires and fishing lines.

SMART WORD

cocoon a silk covering made by some insects

27

Use your SMART WORDS

Read each clue. Choose the Smart Word it describes.

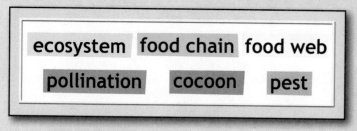

ecosystem food chain food web

pollination cocoon pest

1. It is a living thing that eats farm crops or carries disease.

2. It is the process through which insects help plants with flowers make seeds.

3. It is all of the living and nonliving things in an area.

4. It shows how food flows from one living thing to another in an ecosystem.

5. It shows how one living thing might be eaten by several other kinds of living things in an ecosystem.

6. It is a silk covering made by some insects.

Answers on page 32

Talk Like a Scientist

Your friend wishes that all insects and spiders would just disappear. Use your Smart Words to explain to your friend how they can be helpful.

28

Did You Know?

About 40 different kinds of funnel-web spiders live in the forests of Australia. Some are known for having a deadly venom that acts quickly.

That's Amazing!

These spiders build "trip wires" made of web silk in front of their homes. If an insect trips over the wire, the spider jumps out to grab its meal.

Thanks, Spider!

Researchers are working to use the deadly venom of these spiders to make a pain medicine for humans.

Glossary

abdomen the part of an insect's body that helps it digest food, produce young, and breathe

antennae long, thin structures on an insect's head that are used for feeling and smelling

carnivore an animal that eats only meat

cocoon a silk covering made by some insects

compound eye a structure made up of many separate parts that helps an animal see

ecosystem all of the living and nonliving things in an area

egg an oval or round structure that holds a young animal and the food it needs to develop

exoskeleton a hard covering on the outside of an animal's body

food chain the flow of food from one living thing to another

food web a group of overlapping food chains in a habitat

hatch to break out of an egg

insect an invertebrate animal that has a body with usually three segments, an exoskeleton, three pairs of legs, two antennae, and usually two pairs of wings

invertebrate an animal without a backbone

life cycle the changes an animal goes through from the time it is born until it can produce young

pest any living thing that harms other living things or crops

pollination the movement of pollen from one flower part to another

spider an invertebrate that has a body with two segments, an exoskeleton, eight legs, and does not have wings or antennae

thorax the middle part of an insect's body that has legs and wings attached to it

venom poison produced by an animal

web a net of silk threads that a spider uses to catch insects

Index

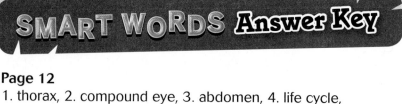

SMART WORDS Answer Key

Page 12
1. thorax, 2. compound eye, 3. abdomen, 4. life cycle,
5. invertebrate, 6. exoskeleton, 7. antennae, 8. insect

Page 20
1. web, 2. hatch, 3. carnivore, 4. spider, 5. venom, 6. egg

Page 28
1. pest, 2. pollination, 3. ecosystem, 4. food chain, 5. food web,
6. cocoon